TCA Think Tank Editions

Crafting Value in Singapore Homes

by TCA Design & Build

Pier Alessio Rizzardi

TCA Design & Build

TCA Think Tank Pte Ltd
20 Depot Road, 109679, Singapore

+65 83814587
info@tcadesignbuild.com

tcadesignbuild.com

Author: Pier Alessio Rizzardi
Editing: TCA Think Tank Editions

© TCA Think Tank Editions.
All rights are reserved.
No parts of this publication may be reproduced, stored in a retrieval system or transmitted, in any form or by any means, electronic, mechanical, photocopying, recording or otherwise, without the prior permission of TCA Think Tank Editions.

Every effort has been made to gain permission from copyright holders and/or Photographer, where known, for images reproduced in this book, and care has been taken to caption and credit those images correctly.

Any omission are unintentional and we will be happy to include appropriate credit in future editions if further information is brought to the publisher's attention.

TCA Think Tank Editions
Books on Architecture

First published in November 2023
by TCA Think Tank Editions
Powered by TCA Think Tank Pte. Ltd.

Singapore: 20 Depot ln, 109763,
Italy: Via Bettinelli, 4, 20136 Milan

www.tcathinktankeditions.com

Printed in UK in 2023
ISBN 978-1-9164537-9-1

Contents

Choosing the Perfect Design & Build Partner in Singapore   4

Architectural Value Maximization   11

The Bondek Revolution   15

Lim Terrace: Modern Fusion   21

Khoo Terrace: Concrete Marvel   31

Ong Terrace: Fresh Privacy   40

Teo Terrace: Black & White Delight   50

27 Shophouse: Cultural Gem   59

Farrer Shophouse: Timeless Treasure   69

De Saedeleer Shophouse: Timeless Treasure   78

Golovkovskaya Condo: Lofted Luxuries   88

Shenton Office: The Art of Workspace   98

Crafting Spaces with Excellence   107

Team and Credits   109

Choosing the Perfect Design & Build Partner in Singapore
5 Steps

In Singapore, a country renowned for its architectural innovation and stringent building codes, embarking on a home renovation project is not merely a matter of aesthetic enhancement but also of regulatory compliance and strategic planning. With a landscape dotted with charming terrace houses and heritage shophouses, each renovation project tells a story of tradition meeting modernity. To navigate this complex process, selecting the right renovation partner becomes paramount. This chapter outlines a strategic approach to identifying a design and build company that not only aligns with your vision but also thrives within the regulatory tapestry of Singapore's construction industry.

Step 1:
Define Your Vision and Budget Understanding Your Needs

Pier Alessio Rizzardi

Renovation in Singapore is not a one-size-fits-all endeavor. Whether it is an A&A project that requires the integration of new elements into an existing structure or a full-scale rebuild, the first step is to have a definitive understanding of your end goal. Visualize your renovated space - is it a modernist haven within the confines of a heritage shophouse, or is it a technologically advanced terrace house equipped with smart home features?

Budgeting with Precision

Alongside vision is the budget. A realistic budget is not just a number; it's a detailed financial plan that considers construction costs, materials (such as the use of I-beams and Bondek for structural support), labor, design fees, and a buffer for unforeseen expenses. Remember, in Singapore's competitive market, cost overruns can be a common plight, and hence, a well-articulated budget is your safeguard.

**Step 2:
Research Companies with Local Expertise: Why Local Expertise Matters**

Singapore's building regulations and climate-specific requirements dictate that your renovation partner must have local expertise. This ensures familiarity with the necessary building materials suited to the tropical climate and an understanding of the Urban Redevelopment Authority's (URA) conservation requirements for shophouses and terrace houses.

Leveraging Reviews & Portfolios

Start with an online search, then dive into the reviews and customer testimonials. A portfolio examination will give you insights into their style and quality of work. Check for before-and-after images, and pay attention to the details, especially in projects similar to yours.

Step 3:
Evaluate Experience with A&A and Detailed Jobs: Importance of Specialization

With a focus on A&A and detailed renovation jobs, experience is non-negotiable. Evaluate potential partners based on their track record with these specific types of projects. Companies like TCA Design & Build not only bring expertise but also a proactive approach to meeting the unique challenges of each project.

Submissions and Approvals

In Singapore, renovations often require multiple submissions for approval, from the initial planning stage to the final building inspection. A company with a history of successful submissions for A&A projects will have a deep understanding of the necessary paperwork and processes, ensuring a smoother renovation journey.

Step 4: Set Up Consultations and Discuss Submissions
The Consultation Process

Personal consultations will allow you to assess the company's communication skills and their understanding of your vision. It's also the time to discuss their process for handling the paperwork and submissions required for building and renovation projects in Singapore.

Evaluating Technical Proficiency

During the consultation, evaluate their technical proficiency. Ask about their experience with the specific construction techniques and

materials you're interested in, such as the use of I-beams and Bondek in structural work, which are common in Singapore for their durability and strength.

Step 5:
Thoroughly Review Contract for Singapore-specific Clauses
Deciphering the Contract

A well-drafted contract is your blueprint for a successful renovation. It should clearly outline the scope of work, timelines, payment schedules, and clauses specific to Singapore's regulations. Look for transparency in terms of material costs, labor charges, and provisions for change orders.

Singapore-Specific Clauses

Ensure that the contract includes clauses that cover local nuances, such as compliance with the Building and Construction Authority (BCA) standards, adherence to URA's conservation guidelines if applicable, and any other Singapore-specific legal requirements.

Final Thoughts

Choosing the right renovation partner in Singapore requires a blend of thorough research, financial planning, and a keen eye for detail. By following these five steps, you position yourself to select a company that not only shares your vision but is also equipped to bring it to fruition within the unique context of Singapore's construction landscape. TCA Design & Build exemplifies such a partnership, offering a synthesis of local knowledge, design expertise, and regulatory fluency that is crucial for any renovation project's success in this city-state.

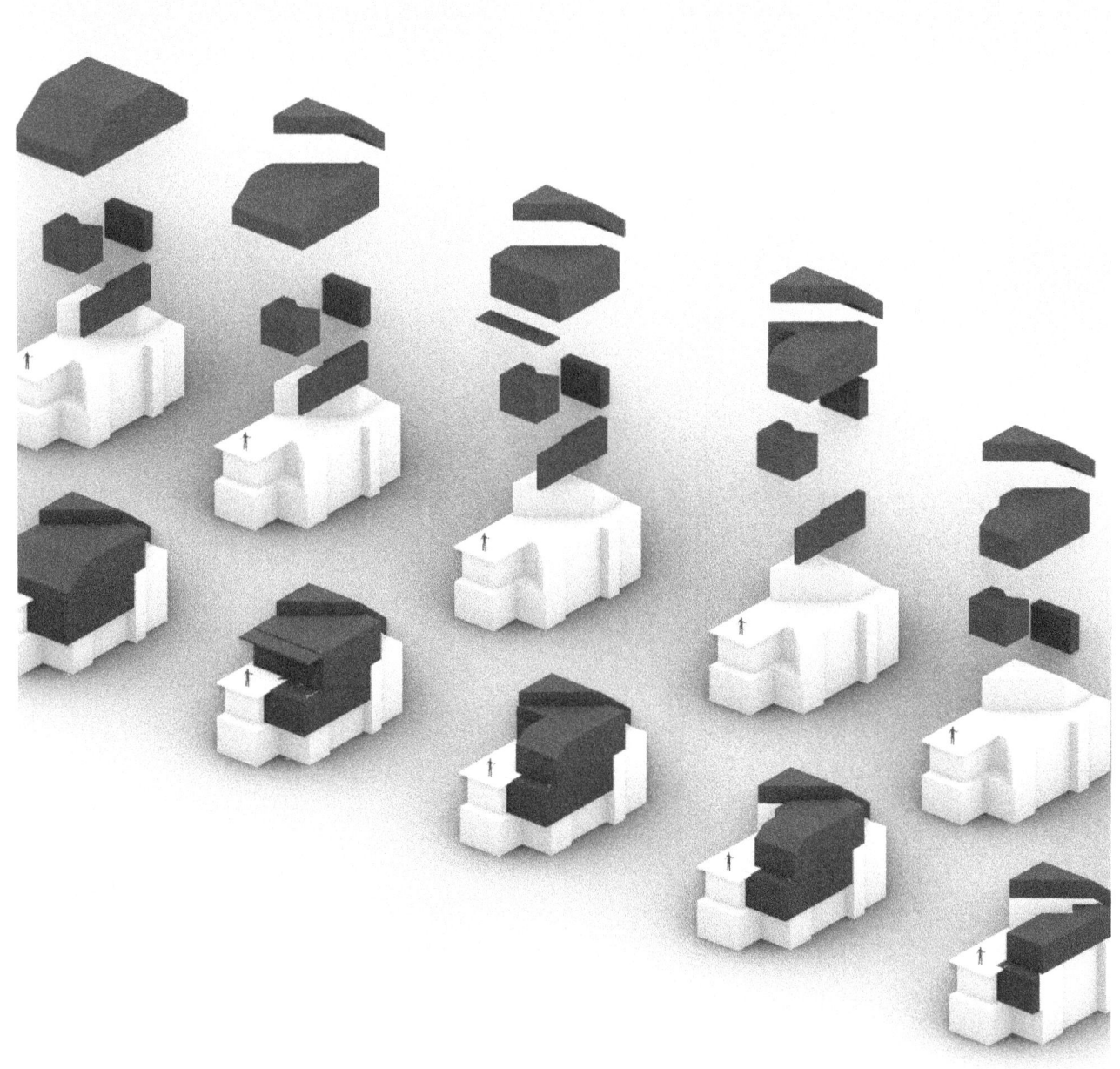

Pier Alessio Rizzardi

Architectural Value Maximization
Singapore's Real Estate Panorama

Singapore's bustling urban landscape offers a dynamic canvas for homeowners to not only create a sanctuary for themselves but also to craft a wise investment that appreciates over time. This chapter is dedicated to unraveling the sophisticated strategy of Gross Floor Area (GFA) enhancement—a method that has become increasingly critical for property owners looking to elevate both their living experience and the fiscal performance of their investments.

Tailoring Homes for Elevated Comfort and Financial Growth

Navigating Singapore's distinctive and lucrative real estate market requires an astute understanding of how to increase property value through design and construction. This section expands on the tactical approach to GFA optimization, outlining the potential for a

30-50% increase in property value. Whether one owns a terrace house, a semi-detached residence, or a sprawling bungalow, this part of the chapter will discuss the essential tactics for maximizing GFA while staying within the URA's regulatory compass.

Terrace Homes: Ingenious Design Solutions for Compact Spaces

Terrace homes in Singapore often require imaginative solutions to make the most of limited space. Here, we delve deeper into the transformative potential of well-planned vertical or horizontal expansions that conform to URA's strict planning guidelines. We'll explore architectural techniques that not only extend living areas but also significantly enhance the property's functionality and market desirability.

The Art of Augmenting Semi-Detached Houses

With a semi-detached house comes the challenge and opportunity to blend individuality with coherence. This section will explore the art and science of executing tasteful extensions or additions that contribute to an increase in usable space and overall property value. It will provide insights into maintaining architectural harmony with existing structures, all while navigating the URA's stringent development protocols.

Bungalows: Redefining Luxury with Strategic Space Enhancement

Bungalows, with their generous land allotment, present a canvas ripe for ambitious GFA enhancements. This part of the chapter will serve as a guide for homeowners to strategically add modern elements and optimize functional space, thereby significantly boosting the property's luxury quotient and market value. It will cover the nuances of design that respect the integrity of the property's original charm while introducing modern amenities.

Mastering the URA's Regulatory Framework for Property Development

To successfully embark on a GFA increase, one must navigate the complexities of the URA's Master Plan. This vital segment of the chapter outlines the procedural roadmap for understanding permissible development intensities and GFA for various property types. Readers will learn about the importance of professional architectural assessments, the intricacies of designing within set regulatory boundaries, and the financial nuances associated with development charges for substantial GFA improvements.

Investing in Design as a Pathway to Enhanced Property Value

Concluding the chapter, we will underscore the fact that investing in the design and construction process is a strategic endeavor with the potential to yield significant financial returns. This section aims to highlight the transformative impact that a detailed, methodical approach to property enhancement can have within the context of Singapore's unique property market. The discussion will also include an overview of a comprehensive visual guide that walks homeowners through these enhancement strategies.

Pier Alessio Rizzardi

The Bondek Revolution
Reinventing Urban Living

Singapore's architectural fabric is characterized by a continuous interweaving of innovation with heritage, a dynamic intersection where tradition meets modernity. At the heart of this evolution lies the challenge of space optimization—a precious commodity in the densely populated urban tapestry of the city-state. The recent introduction of Bondek structural systems by TCA Design and Build marks a significant milestone in this ongoing transformation, particularly for the iconic shophouses and terrace houses that are emblematic of Singapore's residential landscape.

The Emergence of Bondek in Urban Architecture

Bondek, a synergistic composite steel decking system, has emerged as a cornerstone in contemporary construction, particularly suited to Singapore's regulatory environment and construction standards. Its design seamlessly integrates the tensile strength of steel with the robustness of concrete, facilitating the creation of thinner slabs that belie their sturdy nature. This technological leap is not just a matter of structural achievement; it represents a paradigm shift in maximizing urban space without compromising on quality or design integrity.

Five Pillars of Bondek's Transformative Impact

Space Maximization: Bondek's slim profile slabs redefine vertical space allocation, enabling the addition of extra floors within the permissible building height set by Singapore's Urban Redevelopment Authority (URA). This is a game-changer for shophouse and terrace house owners, who can now envision an expanded living area or commercial space without altering the building's external envelope.

Accelerated Construction Timeline: With Bondek, the necessity for extensive temporary shoring and formwork is significantly diminished, streamlining the construction timeline. This efficiency is particularly advantageous within Singapore's fast-paced development sector, where time savings translate directly into fiscal advantages and reduced labor costs.

Design Versatility: The Bondek system accords architects and designers unprecedented freedom to customize interior layouts, unfettered by the constraints traditionally imposed by structural elements. This flexibility ensures that each shophouse or terrace house can be tailored to meet the specific needs and aesthetic preferences of its occupants, all while adhering to the strict building codes and standards overseen by the Building and Construction Authority (BCA) of Singapore.

Cost Efficiency: The amalgamation of reduced construction duration and lesser material requirements with Bondek slabs equates to a cost-effective building process. For property owners, this means an investment that is not only more affordable upfront but also more lucrative in terms of potential property value appreciation.

Enduring Durability: Bondek structures, by virtue of their hybrid composition, offer remarkable longevity and reduced maintenance needs over time. This durability is a significant consideration in Singapore's tropical climate, which can be harsh on building materials.

TCA Design and Build: A Case Study in Innovation

TCA Design and Build exemplifies how contemporary construction methodologies can be adapted to enhance Singapore's unique architectural heritage. Their approach to Bondek integration respects the historic and cultural essence of shophouses and terrace houses, ensuring that any interior transformations do not disturb the storied façades that contribute to the city's character.

Conclusion: Bondek and the Future of Singaporean Spaces

The adoption of Bondek structures

represents a forward-thinking approach to urban redevelopment, one that is in harmony with Singapore's stringent planning and development strategies.

As TCA Design and Build and others continue to push the boundaries of what is possible within the nation's construction industry, Bondek structures stand poised to redefine Singapore's residential and commercial spaces.

They offer a beacon of innovation that does not simply promise more room to live and work but does so with an eye towards sustainability, efficiency, and respect for the past. It is in this melding of old and new that Singapore's future urban landscape will be crafted, ensuring that its buildings are not only fit for today but are adaptable for the generations to come.

Pier Alessio Rizzardi

Pier Alessio Rizzardi

Lim Terrace
Modern Fusion

Singapore

430 sqm

Residential

The Modern Terrace House in Singapore exemplifies contemporary architectural brilliance, spanning a total living space of 430 sqm. This residence distinguishes itself with its notable facade, intricately interspersed with wood inserts, presenting a delightful juxtaposition to the sleek, modern design. Overhead, pergolas cast dappled shadows, lending an air of tranquility and a touch of nature to the structure.

Its terraces and balconies, underlined by the gentle embrace of pergolas, don't just cater to residents' privacy and protection but also provide a picturesque bridge between indoor and outdoor realms. These external spaces, in all their elegance, serve as a retreat to relish the locale's charm.

Venturing inside, the decor announces itself in a classic black and white palette, seamlessly blending functionality with high aesthetic appeal. The generous use of windows ensures the interiors are bathed in ample natural light, bringing forth a sense of spaciousness and openness. This monochromatic scheme, although minimalist, radiates sophistication, providing a serene backdrop to the bustling city outside.

Pier Alessio Rizzardi

In conclusion, the Modern Terrace House in Singapore stands as a beacon of refined contemporary design. Its facade, accentuated with wooden inserts and topped with pergolas, brings a touch of organic warmth to the structure. The harmonious integration of outdoor terraces with the stark black and white interiors showcases an architectural balance that's both striking and inviting. This residence is a testament to the limitless potential of modern architecture, promising its residents an unparalleled living experience.

Pier Alessio Rizzardi

Khoo Terrace
Concrete Marvel

Singapore

440sqm

Residential

The Exposed Concrete Terraced House in Singapore is an exceptional showcase of modern architectural design, boasting a total living space of 440 sqm. The house is immediately recognizable by its bold and striking facade, constructed entirely of exposed concrete, which showcases the industrial aesthetic that is so sought after in contemporary architecture.

The use of terraces and balconies, surrounded by lush greenery, not only offers residents protection and privacy, but it also serves to seamlessly integrate the interior and exterior spaces. The balconies and terraces are not just

Pier Alessio Rizzardi

functional spaces, but they are also designed to be visually appealing and enjoyable, providing the perfect place to soak up the local climate.

The interior spaces are carefully planned, with a focus on functionality and aesthetic appeal. Large windows and doors allow for ample natural light to enter, creating a bright and airy living environment that is both welcoming and visually appealing. The use of greenery on the balconies and terraces not only protects the privacy of the residents but also serves to create a peaceful and serene atmosphere within the home.

In conclusion, the Exposed Concrete Terraced House in Singapore is a true masterpiece of contemporary architectural design. Its striking facade, constructed entirely of exposed concrete, showcases the raw industrial aesthetic that is so sought after in modern architecture. The combination of terraces, balconies, and greenery, serves to seamlessly integrate the interior and exterior spaces, creating a unique and visually appealing living environment that is both functional and aesthetically pleasing. The house is a true testament to the potential of modern architecture, offering residents a living experience that is truly unparalleled.

Pier Alessio Rizzardi

TCA Design & Build

Ong Terrace
fresh privacy

Singapore

362sqm

Residential

Located in the heart of Singapore, Ong Terrace features clean lines, black concrete facade, and a modern style that is reminiscent of colonial architecture. The generous living area of 362 sqm is designed to provide a luxurious living experience for residents.

The building's façade is designed with square shapes, clean lines, and black concrete, which not only creates a modern look but also provides a functional living environment. The balconies and terraces are carefully crafted to blend indoor and outdoor living spaces, allowing residents to take in the stunning views of the city.

As you step inside, you will be welcomed by a dramatic and refined atmosphere. The dark concrete walls create a sense of depth and contrast, and the large windows and doors allow ample natural light to flood into the interior spaces.

The interior design of Ong Terrace is a harmonious blend of form, function, and style. The luxurious spaces include a top-of-the-line kitchen, a master suite with a spa-like bathroom, and a versatile entertainment room. All of these spaces have been designed with comfort in mind, and provide the ultimate in luxury living.

Pier Alessio Rizzardi

The picturesque courtyards offer a peaceful escape for residents, allowing them to relax and take in the beautiful surroundings. The integration of courtyards adds to the indoor-outdoor living experience and elevates the overall luxury of the home.

In conclusion, Ong Terrace exemplifies contemporary design and modern architectural potential. Its distinctive facade, opulent balconies, and elegant interiors create a visually striking and practical habitat. This edifice provides an unparalleled living experience and stands as a modern architectural masterpiece.

Pier Alessio Rizzardi

TCA Design & Build

Teo Terrace
Black & White Delight

Singapore

660sqm

Residential

Pier Alessio Rizzardi

Teo Terrace in Singapore is a remarkable display of contemporary architectural design, featuring a spacious living area of 660 sqm. Its facade is striking and modern, featuring sleek black and white materials that perfectly embody the sought-after industrial aesthetic in contemporary architecture.

The terraces and balconies at Teo Terrace are designed for luxury and privacy, offering seamless indoor-outdoor integration. They are furnished with comfortable seating and stunning views, providing residents with the perfect place to relax in style.

The interior spaces at Teo Terrace have

been carefully planned, with a focus on functionality, luxury, and aesthetic appeal. Large windows and doors allow an abundance of natural light to enter, creating a bright and airy living environment that is both inviting and visually stunning.

The house features numerous luxury spaces, including a spacious living room with a fireplace, a gourmet kitchen equipped with high-end appliances, a master suite with a spa-like bathroom, and a multi-purpose entertainment room. These spaces are designed to provide residents with the ultimate in comfort and luxury. In addition to the balconies and terraces, Teo Terrace

also features luxurious courtyards. These outdoor spaces are perfect for entertaining guests, relaxing in solitude, or enjoying a beautiful view. The use of courtyards at Teo Terrace enhances the indoor-outdoor living experience and adds to the overall luxury of the home.

In conclusion, Teo Terrace is a masterpiece of contemporary architecture in Singapore. Its bold black and white facade, opulent balconies, terraces, and courtyards, along with sophisticated interiors, create a unique and captivating living space that's both practical and beautiful, embodying modern design excellence.

Pier Alessio Rizzardi

27 Shophouse
Cultural Gem

Singapore

460 sqm

Residential

The historical shophouse on Race Course Road is embarking on a journey of transformation, with an ambitious A&A project designed to revitalize its classic structure. This endeavor will not only preserve the architectural integrity of the past but will also introduce a fresh, modern interior layout across its new total area of 460 square meters.

Internally, the redesign will pay homage to the building's historical significance while embracing contemporary design principles. Exposed concrete beams will be featured prominently, adding an industrial yet sophisticated vibe to the space.

Pier Alessio Rizzardi

The flooring will alternate between the warmth of hardwood and the modern edge of polished concrete, providing a varied textural landscape that complements the overall aesthetic inside and outside within the Heritage shophouse.

A striking mezzanine structure will be a focal point of the interior, offering an innovative use of vertical space and creating a unique visual interest. The use of strong, playful colors in the carpentry will weave a narrative of vibrancy and creativity throughout the rooms, breaking the monochrome dominance and injecting life into the space.

Natural light is playing a key role in the revived shophouse, with the installation of multiple skylights in private rooms and common areas, ensuring that the interior spaces are bathed in a soft, diffused glow. This architectural feature not only enhances the spatial quality but also highlights the building's dynamic new elements and the interplay of materials on walls textures, floors hard wood and careful treatment of the conduits. In reimagining this historical edifice, the design marries the timeless appeal of the shophouse with a bold, modern interior, ready to stand as a beacon of heritage and innovation in the heart of Singapore.

Pier Alessio Rizzardi

Pier Alessio Rizzardi

Pier Alessio Rizzardi

Farrer Shophouse
Timeless Treasure

Singapore

1350 sqm

Residential

Embarking on the renovation of the Jalan Besar shophouse co-living complex offers a stimulating endeavor for our innovative design team. We are set on bringing to life a habitat that seamlessly blends practicality with existing aesthetics, all while encapsulating the energetic and trendy spirit of the neighborhood.

Our design strategy involves weaving cutting-edge elements into the historic shophouse settings. While the decorative facade and vintage shutters image are kept intact as a nod to its rich architectural history, we will subtly intersperse elements of the contemporary design. The aim is to

tailor an environment that is adaptive to the inhabitants' needs and exudes a harmonious yet captivating visual appeal.

We will thoughtfully delineate the generous 1350 sqm area into various ensuite rooms and studio apartments, offering a spectrum of choices for potential residents. To stamp a unique identity onto the space, we'll adopt a daring color scheme, majorly favoring varying shades of blue and teal. These serene tones will strike a balance with the industrial-style concrete flooring that will lay the foundation of the complex.

Drawing inspiration from the revived

Bauhaus aesthetic, our design approach will emphasize sharp lines, unadorned simplicity, and user-friendly functionality. The minimalistic attitude towards furniture and fixtures ensures only the most practical and visually appealing pieces are chosen.

Pier Alessio Rizzardi

TCA Design & Build

De Saedeleer Shophouse
Timeless Treasure

Singapore

165 sqm

Residential

Pier Alessio Rizzardi

The shophouse is poised for a significant transformation with an A&A project that ingeniously integrates over 700 square feet of additional space. Utilizing the innovative Bondek structural decking and casting concrete, the building's total area will be increased to 165 sqm.

Inside, the design celebrates the raw beauty of materials with exposed concrete and brickwork, creating an atmosphere that's both edgy and authentic. White structural components and walls act as a visual counterbalance, providing a bright, neutral backdrop that enhances the interplay of light and shadow.

The interior scheme is designed with a minimalist approach, allowing the texture of raw materials to stand out.
This is not just a nod to aesthetic preferences but also a commitment to durability and timeless design. The resulting environment will be one of contrasts: the warmth of brick against the coolness of concrete, the solidity of the structure juxtaposed with open, airy spaces.

This thoughtful redesign ensures that the shophouse remains relevant and functional, catering to the modern needs of its occupants while retaining its unique architectural character.

Pier Alessio Rizzardi

The blend of industrial materials with sleek, white finishes will create a versatile space that's ready to adapt to various uses, be it commercial, residential, or creative studios, infusing the Race Course Road locale with renewed vibrancy and style.

Pier Alessio Rizzardi

TCA Design & Build

Golovkovskaya Condo
Lofted Luxuries

Singapore

73sqm

Residential

The Urban Loft Project, nestled in a vibrant corner of the city, redefines compact luxury in a 73 sqm space, featuring a stunning mezzanine with a sleek black metal structure. This bespoke interior design is centered around a sculptural zigzag staircase, a space-saving piece that doubles as an art installation, leading up to the elevated private quarters.

Beneath the intricate mezzanine, the living area is transformed into a gallery-esque space, boasting a large, bold black and white painting that anchors the room. A selection of carefully curated sculptural hanging pendants cascades down, each emitting a warm glow that highlights the textures and tones of the space. A thoughtful array of interior design lighting solutions ensures every corner is bathed in an inviting ambiance.

The aesthetic appeal is heightened by the exposed ceiling, which adds an industrial yet refined charm, creating a dialogue between raw authenticity and urban sophistication. This narrative of contrast is echoed throughout the loft, with the interplay of light and shadow, modern and vintage, luxury and functionality.

Embracing the art of utilizing every square

Pier Alessio Rizzardi

Pier Alessio Rizzardi

TCA Design & Build

meter, the Urban Loft Project is not just a residence; it's a statement of personal style and architectural ingenuity, all while providing a sanctuary of inspired design in the heart of the city.

TCA Design & Build

Shenton Office
The Art of Workspace

Singapore

190 sqm

Office

Pier Alessio Rizzardi

Our team's endeavor at Shenton Office was to craft a space that epitomized modern elegance and functionality. The centerpiece of our transformation was the sleek metal mezzanine, ingeniously designed to expand the workspace while enhancing the sense of openness and brightness. This feature was integrated with a discerning eye for detail, sporting a finish that not only complements but elevates the office's design narrative with its understated texture and refined sophistication.

Ascending to the mezzanine, the staircases were selected for their dual role as functional elements and embodiments of the office's luxe aesthetic, merging utility with a sculptural finesse. These lead to areas graced with sumptuous hardwood flooring, adding a layer of warmth and texture that enriches the workspace's welcoming ambiance.

The innovative use of glass partitions, alternating between ribbed, clear, and switchable glass, strategically defines the office's four distinct areas. This thoughtful division ensures seamless flow and functional versatility, maintaining a cohesive and interactive environment.

In essence, this workspace is a celebration of our team's commitment to creating

harmonious spaces that marry visual splendor with practicality. It represents a vision realized, where every component is deliberately chosen to contribute to a workspace that not only captivates but also inspires excellence.

Crafting Spaces with Excellence
The TCA Design & Build Journey

TCA Design & Build is a comprehensive design and build company based in Singapore, renowned for its adeptness in architectural rebuilds, interior design, and loft specialization. As Singapore's second-leading design and build firm, TCA is committed to delivering exceptional service and quality, reflected in their extensive portfolio of renovation, A&A (Alterations & Additions), and rebuild projects for both residential and commercial spaces. Their dedicated team is the backbone of TCA's success. Guided by Project Manager Pier, clients are assured a seamless journey through their home interior projects, with Pier overseeing the renovation process and addressing all project queries. Structural integrity and high-quality construction are guaranteed by Engineer Mark, while Architect John ensures that all designs are both aesthetically pleasing and compliant with regulations. Marc, the Construction Manager, ensures excellence and efficiency on-site, while Metal Fabricator Anisur brings precision to every custom metal work. Flooring Specialist Mamun and Wet-work Specialist Masum are pivotal in their respective areas, delivering quality and timely completion of their crafts. Joinery Specialist Joanna brings artistry to wood crafting and cabinetry, ensuring a fine finish to every build.

Specialists in the design and submission processes are integral to TCA's operations, ensuring that every project is not only designed to meet clients' visions but also that all submissions for extensions, changes of use, and new constructions meet Singapore's stringent standards.

They also offer specialized services in electrical and plumbing works to ensure a fully functional and certified system for any new build or renovation.

Clients are encouraged to book an appointment or drop a line to discuss their projects, with TCA's team ready to provide services that fit the unique needs of each project. Their approach is hands-on, with a focus on creating tailored solutions that transform ideas into tangible, artistic realities. They pride themselves on their responsiveness, efficiency, and commitment to customer satisfaction, as evidenced by their positive reviews and testimonials.

TCA Design & Build offers a full spectrum of services, from initial design consultations to the final construction touches, making them

Project manager

Pier will guide you through your home interior journey, sa lead design manager taking charge of the team and oversees the entire renovation process, and answer all queries regarding your project.

Engineer

Mark, a structural design and construction expert, guarantees high-quality work delivered promptly. He ensures every project meets standards and responds swiftly to queries.

Architect

John, an architectural design and planning specialist, ensures top-notch results delivered on time. He ensures each plan complies with regulations and responds quickly to inquiries.

Construction Manager

As a seasoned site supervisor, Marc ensures excellence at every construction phase delivers swiftly, maintains benchmarks, and promptly addresses on-site issues.

Metal Fabricator

As an expert on-site metal fabricator, Anisur ensures excellent craftsmanship in every construction phase, delivers projects promptly, adheres to quality standards, and quickly resolves any work-related concerns.

Flooring specialist

As a skilled flooring specialist, Mamun guarantees exceptional quality in each installation phase, completes assignments on time, maintains high standards of workmanship, and promptly addresses any issues related to the flooring work.

Wet-work specialist

As a skilled on-site concrete specialist, Masum demonstrates exceptional expertise in wet works, screeding, and plastering throughout each stage of building. He completes tasks efficiently, and swiftly addresses any job-related issues.

Joinery specialist

As an adept artisan at Joinary with Joanna, she shows outstanding proficiency in wood crafting, cabinetry, and joinery throughout each phase of construction. She finalizes projects effectively, and promptly tackles any work-related challenges.

our clients

verified

a one-stop-shop for anyone looking to renovate, rebuild, or create from scratch. They invite potential clients to reach out via their contact form, phone, or WhatsApp to begin the transformation of their spaces into dream properties. With a promise of quality, innovation, and a drive to exceed expectations, TCA is poised to maintain and advance their standing as one of the top design and build experts in Singapore.

Embracing the future of construction and design, TCA Design & Build continually adopts the latest technologies and sustainable practices to bring eco-friendly and smart solutions to their projects. Their commitment to innovation is evident in their use of cutting-edge design software and construction techniques, which not only streamline the build process but also minimize environmental impact. By integrating green building concepts and intelligent systems into their projects, TCA ensures that each structure is not just a work of art but also a beacon of modern sustainability and efficiency.

Moreover, TCA's dedication extends beyond the build. They understand that a successful project is one that stands the test of time in both durability and design. This foresight drives their aftercare service, offering maintenance and upgrade advice to ensure that every property remains as functional and visually appealing as the day it was completed. This holistic approach cements TCA Think Tank Design & Build's reputation as not just builders but as custodians of their clients' investments, guaranteeing that every creation is an enduring asset. With TCA, clients do not just build structures; they build legacies. TCA Design & Build, in their pursuit of excellence, extends their focus beyond just construction and design, embracing a profound commitment to nurturing robust community ties and forging strong industry alliances. They recognize the vital role that collaboration plays in the dynamic field of design and construction, especially in today's rapidly evolving landscape. To this end, they actively seek out and engage with a diverse range of local artisans, material suppliers, and cutting-edge technology experts. This approach of collaboration doesn't just infuse their projects with unique, locally-sourced materials and insights, but it also significantly contributes to nurturing the local economy and fostering the growth of local talent.

TCA is deeply involved in knowledge sharing and industry engagement. They frequently conduct workshops, participate in seminars, and are a constant presence in key industry events. Through these platforms, they not only share their rich expertise but also absorb new ideas and trends in the realms of design and construction. This commitment to both teaching and learning keeps them at the vanguard of architectural and design innovation. Such initiatives underscore TCA's dedication not just to their craft, but to the broader community as well. They are more than just a leading design and build firm; they are a socially responsible and dynamic leader, constantly pushing the boundaries in Singapore's design and build sector and contributing positively to its evolution.

www.ingramcontent.com/pod-product-compliance
Lightning Source LLC
Chambersburg PA
CBHW042021090526
44591CB00023B/2923